CHALLENGING MINDS. INSPIRING SUCCESS.

CITY COLLEGE
NORWICH

Please return on or before the last
date stamped below.
Contact: 01603 773 114 or
01603 773 224

A FINE WILL BE CHARGED FOR OVERDUE ITEMS

DO IT YOURSELF

Keeping Fit

Body Systems

Carol Ballard

Heinemann
LIBRARY

www.heinemann.co.uk/library
Visit our website to find out more information about Heinemann Library books.

To order:
☎ Phone 44 (0) 1865 888066
🖹 Send a fax to 44 (0) 1865 314091
💻 Visit the Heinemann bookshop at www.heinemann.co.uk/library to browse our catalogue and order online.

First published in Great Britain by Heinemann Library, Halley Court, Jordan Hill, Oxford OX2 8EJ, part of Pearson Education.

Heinemann is a registered trademark of Pearson Education Ltd.

© Pearson Education Ltd 2008
First published in paperback in 2008
The moral right of the proprietor has been asserted.

Editorial: Louise Galpine and Catherine Veitch
Design: Richard Parker and Tinstar Design Ltd
Illustrations: ODI
Picture Research: Mica Brancic and Elaine Willis
Production: Victoria Fitzgerald

Originated by Chroma Graphics (Overseas) Pte. Ltd
Printed and bound in China by Leo Paper Group.

ISBN 978 0 4311 1 119 3 (hardback)
12 11 10 09 08
10 9 8 7 6 5 4 3 2 1

ISBN 978 0 4311 1 135 3 (paperback)
12 11 10 09 08
10 9 8 7 6 5 4 3 2 1

British Library Cataloguing in Publication Data
Ballard, Carol
Keeping fit : body systems - (Do it yourself)
613.7'1

A full catalogue record for this book is available from the British Library.

Acknowledgements
The publishers would like to thank the following for permission to reproduce photographs: ©Corbis pp. **4** (Steve Chenn), **8** (Bettmann), **27** (Duomo), **29** (Richard T. Nowitz), **43** (Roy Morsch); ©Getty Images pp. **5** (John Kelly), **7** (Tara Moore), **11** (Nick Veasy), **13** (Brad Rickerby), **15** (Allsport Concepts/Mike Powell), **17** (Photographer's Choice/Karl Weatherly), **19** (Taxi/Michael Malyszko), **21** (Johner Images), **30** (Stone/Christel Rosenfeld), **31** (Simon Weller), **32** (Joe McBride), **33** (Allsport Concepts/Pascal Rondeau), **36** (Chris McGrath), **37** (Juergen Stein), **38** (Digital Vision/Roy McMahon), **39** (Vince Michaels), **42** (PhotoDisc); ©PhotoLibrary p. **41**; ©Science Photo Library pp. **9** (D. Roberts), **23** left and right (ISM), **24** (Biophoto Associates), **25** (Susumu Nishinaga).

Cover photograph of woman stretching leg on track, reproduced with permission of Getty Images/Digital Vision.

Every effort has been made to contact copyright holders of any material reproduced in this book. Any omissions will be rectified in subsequent printings if notice is given to the publishers.

The publishers would like to thank Nick Lapthorn for his help in the preparation of this book.

Contents

Any words appearing in the text in bold, **like this**, are explained in the glossary.

Get moving!

Imagine you have just got a new bicycle. You could treat it in one of two ways:

1. Not use it very much, dump it carelessly on the ground, and never clean or oil it.

2. Use it often, put it away carefully, keep it clean and oiled.

Which would keep it looking best and working most efficiently? It would obviously be the second. If you didn't look after your bicycle, you could buy a new one – although it would be expensive. Now think about your body. You can treat it badly or you can take care of it, just as you could a bicycle. But could you go to a shop and buy a new body if it wore out? No! It makes sense to take very good care of your body. You have to keep it in good working condition for the whole of your lifetime.

Swimming is really good for your body – if you cannot swim yet, why not take some lessons and learn?

What sort of exercise?

"Keeping fit" really means looking after your body properly. One of the most important things you can do for your body is to exercise it often. That does not just mean at school in sports lessons, it means being active outside school too. There are all sorts of fun things you can do to keep fit – almost anything that gets your body moving is going to be good for it!

An active body

This book shows you what is happening in your body when you move around and exercise. It explains how your body moves and what your **heart** and **lungs** do. It also shows you how to take care of yourself when you exercise. Read on – and then get moving!

Cycling over rough ground like this makes every part of the body work hard – but it is important to follow every safety precaution!

Warming up

Bend and stretch

You do not need any equipment for these exercises, but make sure you are in a space big enough to swing your arms and legs freely.

1 Waist twists

Stand with your feet about the same distance apart as your shoulders. Put your hands on your hips. Now slowly move your hips round in a circle. Do five circles clockwise then five circles anti-clockwise.

2 Shoulder rolls

Stand as you did for waist twists. Lift your right arm with your hand pointing upwards as high as you can. Now swing your arm backwards, down, forwards, and up to where you started, to draw a complete circle. Do this five times with your right arm then five times with your left arm. Then repeat, but circling your arms in the opposite direction – forwards, down, backwards, and up. Can you move each arm in a different direction at the same time?

3 Leg stretch

Lie on your back on the floor. Keeping your head on the floor, lift your right leg and bring your knee as close to your chest as you can. Then lower your leg to the floor again. Do the same with your left leg. Repeat five times for each leg.

Prepare your body

It is important to prepare your body gently for exercise, rather than giving it a nasty shock! You can do this by spending a few minutes doing some bending and stretching exercises like the ones described here. Gentle activities like this are called "warming up" because as you do them your **muscles** get warmer.

Warming up ideas

Other good warming up activities include:

* gentle jogging
* running on the spot
* hopping
* jumping.

Have you seen professional sportsmen and women doing stretches like this before they begin? Their bodies need to warm up just as yours does.

Avoiding injury

Warming up can help to avoid injury. If your body is cold and stiff when you do something very energetic, you can easily damage muscles and **joints**. Warming up helps muscles and joints to get ready for whatever you need them to do and reduces the chance of damage or injury.

Bones and muscles

To understand how warming up before you exercise can reduce the risk of injury, you need to know how your **bones** and muscles work.

Bone facts

A baby has about 300 bones when it is born. During childhood, some bones join together. An adult skeleton is made up of 206 bones of all sorts of shapes and sizes. The smallest bones are in the ear. The longest bone is the **thigh** bone.

This gymnast needs a flexible spine to bend her body into this shape!

Bones

Your bones provide a framework for the rest of your body – without your bony **skeleton**, you would be a jelly-like lump! The backbone (**spine**) is made up of 33 separate bones. These all link together to make a **flexible** central support. Because the backbone is flexible, you can bend over and touch your toes. Some of your bones protect delicate parts of your body. The skull protects your brain. The **ribcage** protects the **heart** and **lungs**.

If you could see your skeleton when you kick a ball, it would look like this.

Muscles

Muscles are important too. Without them, we would not be able to move at all. They are like stretchy **elastic** bands and most are attached to bones. The muscles pull the bones into new positions, allowing us to move. Sometimes you want to move part of your body while the rest stays still, such as when you hit a ball. At other times you want to move all of your body, such as when you run. It does not matter what type of movement it is – every movement needs muscles!

Muscle facts

Humans have around 650 muscles! The smallest muscle is in the ear. The longest muscle is at the front of the thigh. One of the strongest muscles moves the hip and thigh when you jump or climb.

Cold muscles

Before you begin exercising your muscles are cold. They are not very elastic, which means they are not very stretchy. If you start to exercise vigorously when your muscles are like this, you can easily stretch them too much. This can tear them. A torn muscle is a painful injury and the damage can take a long time to heal. This is one good reason for warming up gently before you start your exercise activity. Gentle stretching exercises help to warm the muscles up slowly. This means they are ready to stretch a lot when you begin to be very active.

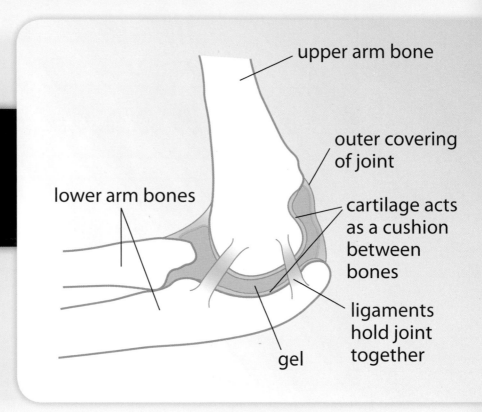

This picture shows how the parts of the elbow joint all fit together.

upper arm bone

outer covering of joint

cartilage acts as a cushion between bones

lower arm bones

ligaments hold joint together

gel

Inside a joint

Caring for your joints is another good reason for warming up before you exercise. If you could look inside a joint, you would see that it has several parts:

- an outer covering
- the ends of the two bones that meet at the joint
- **cartilage** covering the ends of each bone to stop them rubbing against each other
- tough bands called **ligaments** that hold the joint together
- a jelly that acts like lubricating oil in an engine.

Joints

A joint is the place where two bones meet. Elbows, wrists, knees, and ankles are all joints. You cannot bend a bone itself, but you can bend at the joint between two bones. Without joints you would be very stiff. Imagine how difficult it would be to walk without bending your knee or ankle. Some joints only allow movement in one direction. Your knee is like this – you can only bend it backwards and forwards. Other joints allow movement in all sorts of directions. Your shoulder is like this – you can move your upper arm in almost any direction you want to.

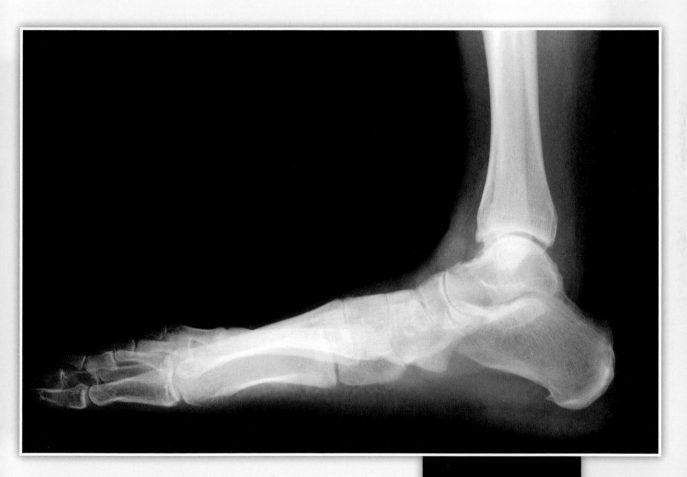

This X-ray shows the bones in an ankle joint.

Loosening up

Before you exercise, the jelly inside your joints is quite firm and your joints are stiff. As you get warmer the jelly gets runnier and your joints can move more easily. Gentle warming-up exercises before you begin help to warm the jelly making your joints feel loose and supple.

Move around, have fun

Steps to follow

Skip!

For this activity you will need:

* a skipping rope
* plenty of space.

Before you start, check your rope is the right length for you. Stand on the middle of it and hold each end up. The ends should just come to your armpits. If your rope is shorter than this, you need a different one. If it is longer than this, tie a knot in one or both ends to shorten it.

1 Hold the end of your skipping rope in each hand. As you turn the rope, step over it with your right foot on one turn and then your left foot on the next turn. You can do this on the spot or can travel over a distance.

2 Now turn the rope and jump over it with both feet together every time. You can vary this by doing an extra little bounce between each jump, or by jumping with your feet together on one turn then feet apart on the next turn.

3 Do the same as in 1 or 2 but turn the rope backwards instead of forwards.

Keeping fit on your own

There are many different things you can do on your own to keep fit and have fun. Here are some ideas:

- Go for a walk – this is so simple but walking briskly is really good for you. For a change try walking 50 paces then jogging 50 paces.

- Go swimming – it exercises most of the **muscles** in your body.

- Ride your bicycle – why not cycle to local places instead of going by bus or car?

- Dance – put your favourite music on and make up your own dance steps.

- Hula hoop – how many times can you spin a hula hoop around your waist before it falls to the floor?

- Ball games – find a wall, practise throwing a ball against it and catching it. Make it harder by turning round in between throwing and catching, or try clapping your hands behind your back.

- Basketball – shoot a ball through a basketball net and jump to catch it.

Circle ball game

For this activity you will need:

* a ball

* five or more people.

This activity is good for improving catching and throwing skills and you have to stay alert all the time!

1 Stand in a circle, spacing yourselves by spreading your arms out so that your fingertips touch the fingertips of the person on each side of you.

2 One person holds the ball. They throw it quickly to somebody else, shouting that person's name as they throw.

3 The person whose name is called must catch the ball and then throw it quickly to somebody else, shouting that person's name as they throw. If the catcher drops the ball, they are out.

4 The game continues until only two people are left.

5 The aim is to keep the ball moving as quickly as you can, for as long as you can.

Keeping fit with friends

You and your friends can have great fun keeping fit together! Team games such as basketball, football, and hockey are played at many schools. There are lots of sports clubs to join out of school, too, where you can improve your basic skills and play in matches and tournaments.

Have you ever tried running in a relay race like this? Organized sports are great fun and can help you to keep fit.

As well as organized sports, there are other ways of keeping fit with your friends. Set yourself these challenges:

Activity	What you need	What you do
Set a challenge, such as how far can you travel without putting your feet on the floor	Place such as gymnasium, activity centre, or adventure playground	See if you can achieve the challenges
Skip rope together	Long skipping rope	Two people turn a long rope, others take it in turns to skip
Make up a series of simple exercises, such as touch your toes, do star jumps, sit down and stand up	Space large enough to move around freely	All start together and see who can complete the series fastest, or do the most repeats in a set time
Play a game such as tag	Plenty of space for running around	One person is "It", and tries to catch somebody else; everybody else runs away to avoid being caught – but if you are caught you become "It" instead

Feel your muscles work

1 Hold your right arm out straight. Make the hand into a fist with the palm upwards.

2 Lightly rest the fingers of your left hand on the front of your right upper arm.

3 Slowly bend your right arm at the elbow and then lower it again. Your left hand should be able to feel the muscles inside your right arm moving as you raise and lower it.

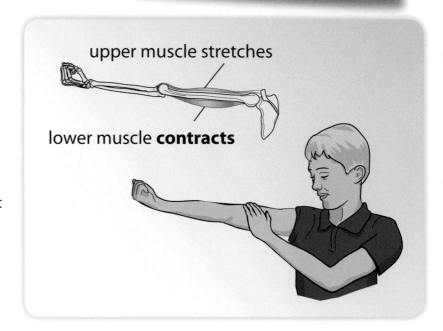

upper muscle stretches

lower muscle **contracts**

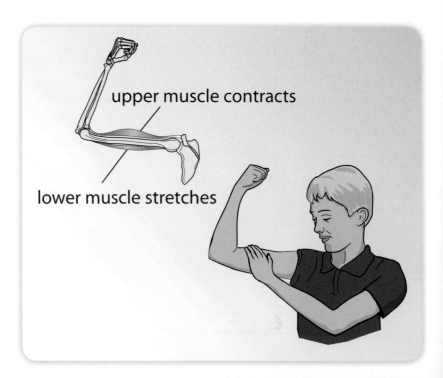

upper muscle contracts

lower muscle stretches

What happens inside your arm?

What is happening inside your arm when you raise and lower it? Two muscles work as a pair, doing opposite jobs.

Raising your arm

When you want to raise your arm your brain sends a signal to the muscle at the front of your upper arm. The signal travels from the brain to the muscle via nerves. When the muscle receives the signal it responds by contracting (getting shorter). The muscle is attached to the **bones** in the lower arm. When it contracts, these bones are pulled up. This also stretches the muscle at the back of the upper arm.

Lowering your arm

When you lower your arm, your brain sends a signal to the muscle at the back of your upper arm. When the muscle receives the signal it responds by contracting (getting shorter). The muscle is attached to the back of the bones in the lower arm. When it contracts, it pulls these bones downwards. This also stretches the muscle at the front of the upper arm.

Cycle races can last a long time and cover great distances. Cyclists' leg muscles are very strong and powerful.

Pairs of muscles

Muscles work in pairs like this to move all the bones in your body. If one muscle pulls a bone in one direction there will be another muscle to pull it back again. When one muscle in a pair contracts to pull the bone the other muscle is stretched.

Pumping blood

Steps to follow

Find your pulse rate

For this activity you will need:

* a clock or watch that shows minutes and seconds.

1 Hold your right hand out with your palm facing up.

2 Gently rest the index and middle fingers of your left hand on the inside of your arm, in line with your thumb and a little above your wrist.

3 Your left hand fingers should be able to feel a regular "beat" in your arm. If you cannot feel anything at first, try moving your left hand fingers around a little until you can. Each beat you feel is one push from your **heart** as it pumps blood round your body.

When you can feel the beat, count how many beats you feel in one minute. This is called your **pulse rate**.

Heartbeats

Your heart beats about 70 times every minute when you are resting, and more when you are moving around and exercising. That makes about:

* 4,000 beats every hour
* 100,000 beats every day
* 40 million beats every year!

The heart

Your heart is mainly made of **muscle**. It is in the middle of your chest, inside your **ribcage**. Your heart's job is to pump blood around your body. It starts pumping even before you are born, and does not stop until you die. You do not have to think about it — your heart keeps on pumping every minute of the day and night.

Blood vessels

Blood travels through a network of tubes called **blood vessels**. The biggest tubes are called **arteries** and **veins**. The tiniest tubes are called **capillaries**.

Medical staff often measure a patient's pulse rate. This can help them to see how well the patient is.

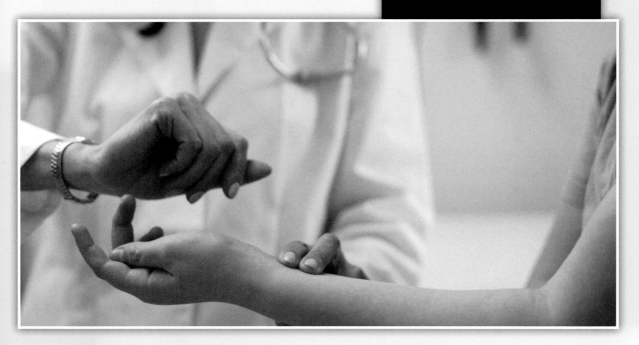

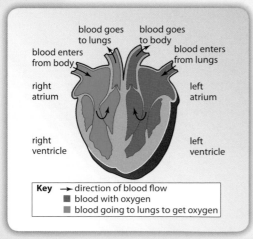

blood goes to lungs
blood goes to body
blood enters from body
blood enters from lungs
right atrium
left atrium
right ventricle
left ventricle

Key → direction of blood flow
■ blood with oxygen
■ blood going to lungs to get oxygen

The movement of blood

Your heart is really like two separate pumps. Veins bring blood from the rest of your body to the right side of your heart. The right side of the heart pumps this blood to the **lungs**. The blood travels through the lungs, where it gets rid of **carbon dioxide** and picks up **oxygen**. It then travels back to the left side of the heart. The left side of the heart then pumps the blood out to the rest of the body. This movement of blood around the body is called **circulation**.

Does your heart rate change when you exercise?

You need a clock or watch that shows minutes and seconds.

1 Begin by sitting quietly and still for five minutes, then measure your pulse rate. Write it down. This is your **resting rate**.

2 Exercise energetically for two minutes. Star jumps or running on the spot are both ideal.

3 As soon as your two minutes are up, measure your pulse rate again. Write it down. This is your after-exercise rate.

4 Sit quietly and measure your pulse rate after another two minutes, and then another five minutes.

5 You can show your results on a graph like this. Get your friends to do the same and add their results to your graph.

You should find that your after-exercise pulse rate was a lot faster than your resting rate. After resting for a while, it should go back to the resting rate again.

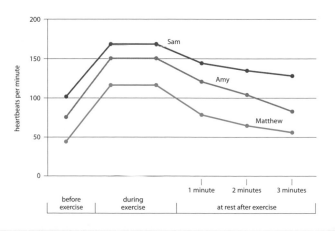

Exercise and pulse rate

Why does this happen? It's all to do with the body supplying your muscles with what they need to work. Blood carries oxygen, energy, and important chemicals around your body. It also collects waste gases and waste chemicals so they can be broken down and removed from the body.

When you are sitting quietly your heart beats just fast enough to give your muscles as much oxygen and energy as they need. When you begin to move or exercise your muscles need more oxygen and energy. They also make more waste gas and chemicals. Your heart pumps faster to make the blood circulate more quickly. This supplies the muscles with extra oxygen and energy, and takes away the waste products.

When you are really active like this girl your heart has to beat faster to pump blood more quickly around your body.

When you rest your muscles need less oxygen and energy. They make less waste. The whole process slows down again. After a few minutes everything is back to normal. The fitter you are, the quicker your pulse rate will return to its normal resting rate.

Breathing

How much does your chest expand?

For this activity you will need:

* a tape measure
* a friend to help you.

1 Ask a friend to put a tape measure around your chest just below your armpits. It should be quite tight around your body but should not squash you at all. Breathe out as much as you can. Your friend should write down the measurement given on the tape measure.

2 Now take the biggest breath you can. Your friend should write down the measurement given on the tape measure again.

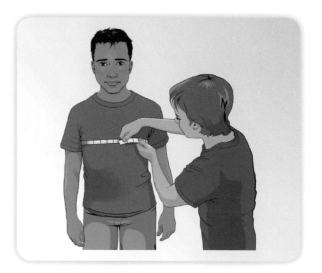

3 Take your first measurement away from your second measurement. This tells you how much your chest expanded when you breathed in.

4 Here is an example of what your results might look like:

First measurement – breathing out 76 cm (30 in)

Second measurement – breathing in 84 cm (33 in)

Take 76 cm (30 in) away from 84 cm (33 in): answer = 8 cm (3 in).

Where are your lungs?

Your **lungs** are in your chest protected by your **ribcage**. When you breathe in they **expand** as they fill up with air. When you breathe out they **contract** as air leaves them. Your lungs cannot do this all by themselves – **muscles** have to help. A big sheet of muscle called the **diaphragm** stretches across the lower part of your chest. Other muscles are attached to your ribs.

The blue areas on this X-ray show a person's lungs. In the first picture, the lungs look big because the person is breathing in. In the second picture, the lungs look smaller because the person is breathing out.

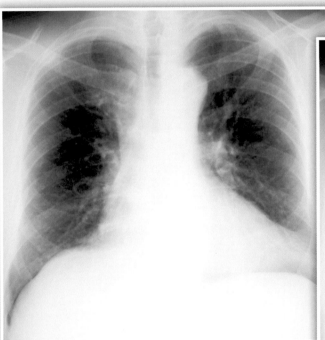

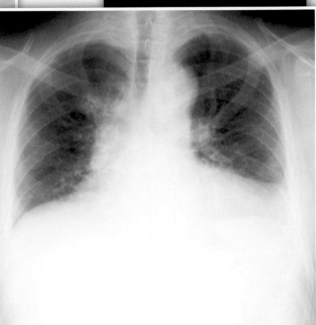

When you breathe in the muscles make the space in your chest bigger. Air is pulled into your body through your mouth and nose. It moves into a tube called the **windpipe** and travels down to the top of your chest. Here, the windpipe branches into two smaller tubes – one carrying air to your left lung and the other carrying air to your right lung.

When you breathe out the opposite happens. The muscles make the space in your chest smaller. This pushes waste air out of your lungs. It is forced out of your lungs into the tubes, then into the windpipe. It leaves your body through your mouth and nose.

A lungful of air

An adult's lungs can hold about 6 litres (11–12 pints) of air. A child's lungs do not hold quite as much as this. Each time you breathe in and out, about 0.5 litres (1 pint) of air enters, then leaves, your lungs.

Inside your lungs

Have you ever wondered what your lungs are like inside? It might seem strange, but try to imagine an upside-down tree. From the top you have a single trunk. This splits into two big branches, then each of the branches splits again and again, into smaller and smaller branches until you come to the tiniest twigs. Your windpipe is like a hollow tree trunk. It splits into two main tubes. Then each of these splits again and again into narrower and narrower tubes. Eventually they form tiny little groups like hollow bunches of grapes. The "grapes" are called **alveoli**. They have very thin walls that gases can pass through. The alveoli are surrounded by tiny **blood vessels**.

This photograph shows part of the inside of a lung. In the centre of the picture is a **bronchiole**. The spaces around it are alveoli.

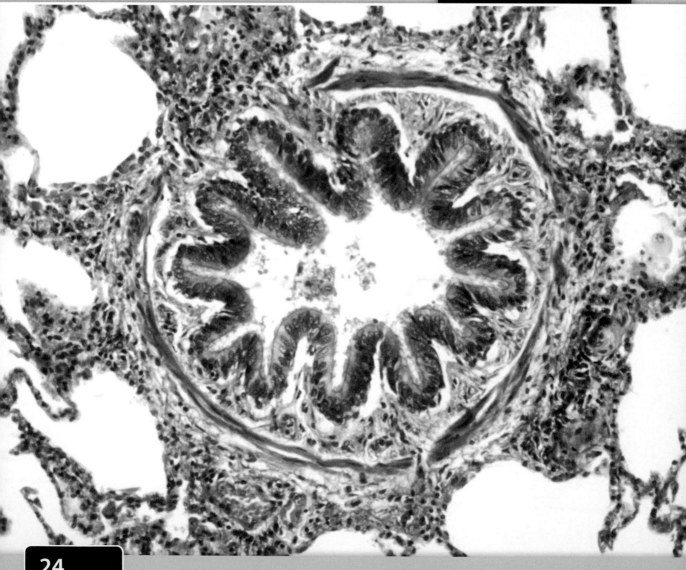

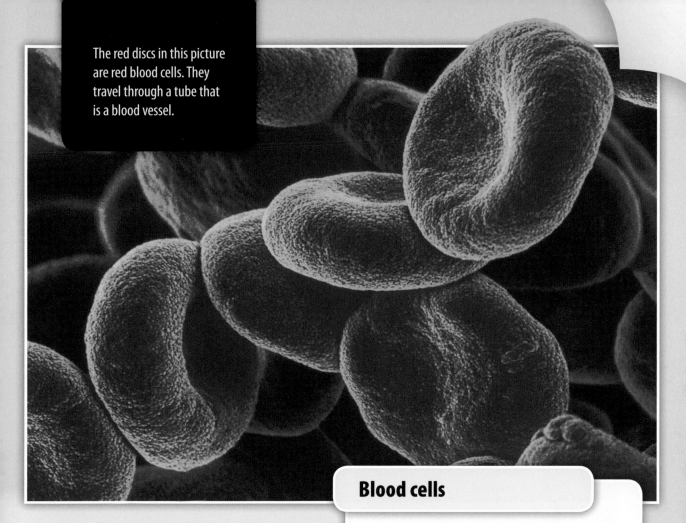

The red discs in this picture are red blood cells. They travel through a tube that is a blood vessel.

Blood cells

How do lungs work?

What actually happens inside your lungs when you breathe in and out?

Breathing in:

Air rushes into the windpipe through the narrower and narrower tubes until it reaches the alveoli. Here, **oxygen** moves through the alveoli walls and into the blood vessels. The blood then carries the oxygen away.

How does oxygen travel in the blood? If you looked at a drop of blood under a microscope, you would see lots of tiny objects floating around in a clear liquid. These are blood **cells**. Some are colourless, but others are red. The red blood cells are what make your blood look red. They are really important because they carry the oxygen around. Carbon dioxide travels around in the liquid.

Breathing out:

Your muscles and other parts of your body make a waste gas called **carbon dioxide**. Your body has to get rid of this somehow. As blood travels around your body it collects waste carbon dioxide. When it reaches the lungs, the carbon dioxide leaves the blood and moves into the alveoli. When you breathe out the waste carbon dioxide is forced out of your body.

Steps to follow

You do not need any equipment for this deep-breathing exercise. It is a good way to begin and end an exercise session.

1 Stand with your feet about the same distance apart as your shoulders. Look straight ahead and let your arms hang down loosely by your sides. Take a very slow, deep breath in while you count to five.

2 Hold your breath for a slow count of two.

3 Let your breath out very slowly as you count to five.

4 Slowly count to two.

Repeat ten times from the beginning.

Automatic or controlled?

Most of the time, you breathe in and out without thinking about it. Your brain automatically controls how fast you breathe. When you are doing some activities, though, it can be important to control your breathing. Swimmers need to breathe in a rhythm that matches their swimming strokes. In breaststroke, when the hands push forwards the head dips under the water. When the hands push back the head lifts out of the water. The swimmer can only take a breath when their head is out of the water.

This swimmer is taking a quick breath as she raises her arm. If she gets the timing wrong she'll get a mouth full of water instead of air!

Slow or fast?

Slow, deep breathing is much more efficient than fast, shallow breathing. This is because, when you breathe slowly and deeply, most of the air taken in gets right down into your lungs. Your body can make full use of the oxygen in every breath. If your breaths are quick and shallow, much of the air does not get any further than your nose or windpipe – so your body cannot get any oxygen from it!

Hold your breath!

Have you ever tried to see how long you can hold your breath for? Take a deep breath in and hold it for as long as you can. Eventually you have to breathe out. This is because your body needs a regular oxygen supply. If you try to stop it by holding your breath, your brain makes you breathe whether you want to or not!

Look after yourself!

Mixing it up

You need a step that will make your **heart** and **lungs** work hard for this activity:

1 Use a bottom stair or step. Step on to it with your right foot first then bring your left foot up too. Then step back down, again with your right foot first.

2 Repeat five times.

3 Repeat five more times using your left foot first.

4 If you can, repeat all this again.

You do not need any equipment for this stretching activity:

1 Stand with your feet about the same distance apart as your shoulders. Hold your hands together straight above your head. Keeping your eyes fixed ahead of you, very slowly bring your arms and upper body down and right round in a big circle until you are back in your starting position.

2 Repeat, but make the circle in the opposite direction.

3 Repeat steps 1 and 2 four more times.

Interval training

Most sportsmen and women combine two different types of exercise in a training session:

- a fast, energetic exercise that really makes the heart work hard
- a slower exercise that doesn't make the body work too hard.

Putting two contrasting exercises together like this is called **interval training**. A simple type of interval training is to sprint 20 paces then walk 20 paces.

While your body is growing and developing, it is a good idea to try to sleep for at least eight hours every night.

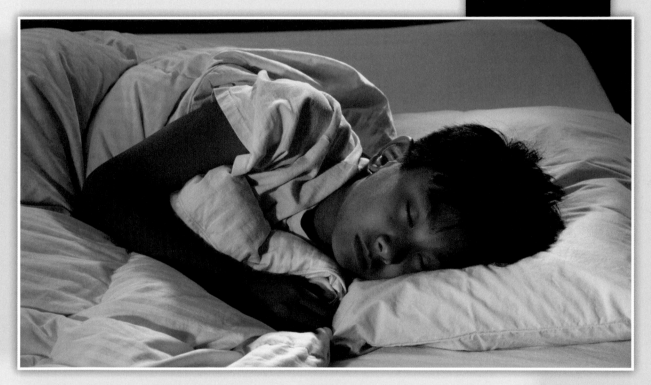

How much exercise?

Everybody is different so it is difficult to give an exact figure for how much exercise you need to do. For most children, an hour of exercise a day is a good starting amount. If you try to do too much exercise your body will get too tired.

Rest and sleep

Rest is important. A good night's sleep will help you to be at your best the next day. If you have too little sleep you will be tired the next day. Your reactions will be slow and your movements will not be as fast and strong as they are when you are properly rested.

Why do you need food?

Whatever you do to keep fit you will use up energy. You get your energy from your food, so it is important to make sure that your food provides enough energy for everything you do. The parts of your food that give you energy are called **carbohydrates** and **fats**. Your food also provides the **proteins** that your body needs to grow and repair, and **vitamins** and **minerals** that keep you healthy.

The best thing about fruit is that, as well as being good for you, it is delicious!

What is in your food?

Different foods provide different things. This table shows you some foods that are good sources of each type of **nutrient**:

Nutrient	Needed for	Found in
Carbohydrates (sugars and starches)	Energy	Bread, pasta, cereal, rice, potatoes
Fats	Energy	Dairy products, nuts, oils, meat
Proteins	Growing and repairing	Meat, fish, eggs, nuts, dairy products
Vitamins and minerals	Staying healthy	Fruit, vegetables

Healthy eating

To stay fit and healthy, and to have plenty of energy for activities, you should try to eat something from each of the groups of food opposite every day. The main part of a meal should be bread, pasta, or cereal, with lots of vegetables or fruit. We should have less protein-rich food, and even less fatty or sugary food.

If you eat more energy-rich food than your body uses up, your body will store the extra food as fat. If you get fat you will find it harder to run around and be active. It is also not good for your **heart**. If you eat less energy-rich food than your body uses up, your body will use the fat it has stored. This can make you feel tired and weak.

Junk food

You have probably heard people talking about "junk foods". Most junk foods contain far more fat, salt, or sugar than your body can use. You should only eat foods such as burgers, chips, and chocolate as a treat every now and then.

Eating junk food like this every day is not good for your body.

Take care of yourself

There are some basic steps you can take to look after yourself, whatever activity you choose to do:

- Protective clothing: Make sure you always wear the right protective clothing for your activity. It is designed to prevent you hurting yourself. For example, cycle helmets protect your head when you are cycling.

- Other clothing: Try to dress sensibly for your activity. Ask yourself questions such as: Are my shoes suitable? Am I likely to be too hot or too cold?

- Equipment: If you have special equipment for your activity check it carefully to make sure it is safe to use. For example, check your bicycle's tyres, brakes, and lights before you set off.

It is easy to tumble when you are skateboarding. The protective clothing this boy is wearing should save him from hurting his head, elbows, or knees.

- Rules and instructions: Most activities have rules or instructions that you should follow. These are for your safety as well as the safety of other people. Breaking the rules or ignoring instructions can put you and others in danger. For example, a bad tackle in a football match can injure your opponent and result in you being sent off!

- Safety notices: Always look for safety notices before you begin. These can give you important information such as where the fire exit is or which is the deep end of the swimming pool.

Oh dear! Because he has broken the rules, this footballer is going to miss the rest of the match.

- Avoid risks: It might sound obvious, but try not to take any unnecessary risks!

- Medical: Some illnesses or conditions mean that you must keep your medicine with you. For example, many people with asthma must keep their inhaler with them. If this applies to you, make sure you do as you have been told to. It is a good idea to also tell an adult who is with you so that they know what to do if you become ill.

Drugs and sport

Steps to follow

Whatever your sport, you do not need **drugs** to improve your performance. Instead, you should practise your skills and be proud of your achievements. Here are some activities to help you improve your skills. These activities are useful in many different sports.

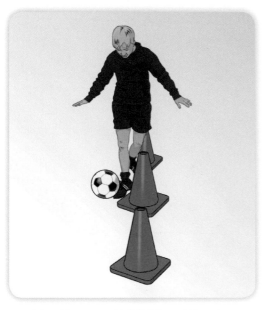

1 Set up several markers in a straight line with spaces between them. Dribble a ball in and out between the markers. Try to keep the ball under your control all the time. Now vary the distance between the markers.

2 Stand several paces back from a wall. Use a tennis racket to hit a tennis ball at the wall. Keep hitting it back when it bounces back to you. How many times can you do it without missing? Use forehand, backhand, and alternate the two. Now try hitting the ball before it bounces each time.

Bounce a basketball on the ground several times. How many bounces can you do without losing control of the ball? Now try bouncing using alternate hands. You can make the practice harder by bouncing the ball under one leg, under the other leg, or behind you.

Banned drugs

Newspapers and television news programmes often have reports about sportsmen or women taking drugs or failing drug tests. There are very strict rules about taking drugs in sport and competitors are tested regularly. In many sports, if someone is found to have taken a banned substance they are not allowed to compete again for a long time.

Taking drugs is cheating!

Taking drugs is really just cheating. The person thinks they are not good enough to win by their own skills so they rely on a drug to help them. This is not fair on the other competitors who have not taken drugs.

Dangers of drugs

Taking drugs to improve your performance is not only unfair it is also very dangerous. Many drugs can damage your body causing health problems for the rest of your life.

Temperature control

When you are active, your **muscles** work hard. They get warm and generate heat. This makes your whole body feel warm. This is fine, but you cannot keep on getting hotter and hotter! Your body has to maintain a constant, safe temperature.

One way your body loses unwanted heat is by sweating. Sweat is a salty liquid made in **sweat glands** in your skin. When you start to get hot, sweat trickles out through tiny holes in the skin called **pores**. As air passes over your skin the sweat evaporates. This helps to cool your skin down. When you stop exercising your muscles stop generating heat. Your body slowly cools down and your skin stops releasing sweat.

This tennis player is wearing a towelling band around his wrist. It will soak up his sweat and stop it dripping on to his racket and making his hand slippery.

Water loss

If you lose a lot of water as sweat your body can become short of water. This is called **dehydration**. It makes your body start to overheat and you might get a headache, feel tired, and thirsty. You might also feel a bit dizzy and faint. You can avoid becoming dehydrated by drinking plenty of water before, during, and after exercise. During exercise you should try to have a drink of water about every 20 minutes, even if you do not feel very thirsty.

Sweating

You have about 3 million sweat glands in your body!

An adult who is very active in a hot environment can lose 2–3 litres (4–6 pints) of sweat in 1 hour!

When you have been exercising hard like this girl, a drink of cold water will cool you down. It will also replace some of the water lost by sweating.

Blood and temperature

Your blood also helps to control your body temperature. A network of tiny blood **capillaries** runs throughout your skin. Some are close to the surface. Others are deep inside the skin.

This athlete's flushed face shows he is really hot! He is pouring cold water over his face to try to cool down.

Getting hot

When your body is resting, blood flows evenly through the skin capillaries. When you start to get hot, more blood flows through capillaries just below the surface of your skin. Heat passes from the blood, through the skin, and into the air. This explains why you often have a red face when you have been exercising hard. There is more blood than usual near the surface of the skin and so it looks red.

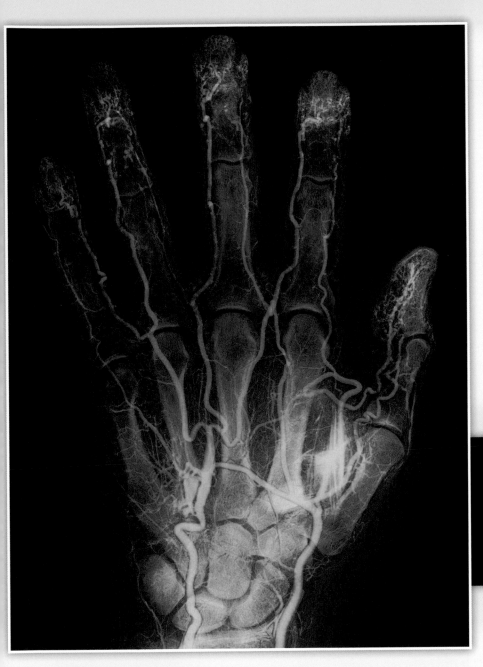

Cooling down

When your body cools down the opposite happens. More blood flows through capillaries deeper in the skin. There is less blood flowing just below the skin's surface so less heat is lost through the skin. If you get very cold, your skin can start to look blue. This is because you cannot see the red colour of the blood as it flows deeper within the skin.

In this X-ray, you can see some of the blood vessels in a hand.

Help your body!

It makes sense to help your body to control its temperature. You can do this by wearing more than one layer of clothes. This will mean you are warm enough when you begin exercising. When you get hot you can take off the top layer. Splashing cold water on your skin or running your wrists (where **blood vessels** are near to the surface of the skin) under a cold tap will help you cool down too. Taking a short break and resting for a few minutes also gives your body a chance to cool down.

When your activity is over...

It is a good idea to cool down slowly rather than to stop suddenly. You do not need any equipment for these activities:

1

Side bends:
Stand with your feet about the same distance apart as your shoulders. Put your hands on your hips. Now slowly bend to your left from your waist, letting your hips move to your right a little. Straighten up and then slowly bend to your right. Repeat several times.

2

Walking around:
It may sound very simple, but walking around slowly for a few minutes can help your body to cool down.

3

Jogging:
If you have been running fast, jogging can be a good way to finish your activity session. You can jog slowly and gently on the spot or over a short distance.

Avoiding muscle stiffness

Cooling down properly after an activity session is as important as warming up before you begin! If you stop exercising suddenly and simply rest, your **muscles** will probably feel stiff and tired the next day. This is because of a substance called **lactic acid**. Your muscles produce lactic acid when they work hard. If your muscles stop exercising suddenly, they cannot get rid of the lactic acid. Some gets trapped in your muscles making them feel tired and heavy. If you do some gentle cooling down exercises, your muscles can slowly get rid of the lactic acid so you feel fine later.

Gentle stretching and bending can help your muscles to cool down after exercise.

Tracksuit time

While you are active, your body will be quite hot. As soon as you stop it will cool down. Try to pull on some warm clothing such as a tracksuit to avoid cooling too much and feeling shivery.

Hygiene

Don't forget about personal hygiene! If you have been active, you will probably have been sweating. A warm shower will get rid of this and clean your skin. It will also help to relax your muscles.

Conclusion

You should now know that keeping active really matters! Being active is one of the best ways of keeping your body fit and healthy.

Strong heart

Exercising a **muscle** makes it stronger. Your **heart** is a muscle, and the more exercise you take the stronger it gets. This means that the more active you are the stronger and healthier your heart will be. You will be able to run faster and keep going for longer.

Have fun!

Exercise and activity should be fun! There are lots of great ways to exercise – both on your own or with friends. This book gives some suggestions, but you will probably have some favourites of your own as well. It is a good idea to vary what you do. Mixing activities that make you run and jump with others that make you bend and stretch will help every part of your body.

The 4 "S's"

A good mix of exercises and activities will help you develop the "4 S's" – Speed, **Stamina**, Strength, and Skills. Together these will help you do well in just about every sport or activity you can think of!

Eating healthy food like this provides your body with everything it needs to be active and fit.

Be sensible

Being sensible about your exercise is important. Before you start, check with an adult that your planned activity is safe for you. Also try to remember to:

- warm up before you exercise
- cool down when you finish
- wear protective clothing if necessary
- obey signs, rules, and instructions.

These young basketball players need the "4 S's" to play well.

Eat, drink, and sleep

Keeping fit is not only about exercise, though. Other things are involved, too, including:

- eating healthy food with plenty of fresh fruit and vegetables
- drinking plenty of water
- getting a good night's sleep.

If you can combine exercise, rest, and a healthy diet you are well on the way to having a fit, healthy body. Your hair will shine, your skin will be clear and fresh, your eyes will be bright, and you will feel ready for anything!

Glossary

alveoli very tiny part of your lungs. Several alveoli together look like a very, very small bunch of grapes.

artery type of blood vessel. Arteries are the strongest blood vessels.

blood vessel name for part of the network of tubes through which blood travels round your body. All your blood vessels together make up a complicated network that reaches every part of you.

bone part of your skeleton. Your bones give your body its shape.

bronchiole small branch of air tube in the lungs. Bronchioles look like the roots of a tree.

capillary type of blood vessel. Capillaries are the smallest blood vessels.

carbohydrate type of food chemical or food group. Carbohydrates contain a lot of energy and provide fuel for the body. Pasta, rice, and bread all contain carbohydrates.

carbon dioxide waste gas made by your body. Carbon dioxide leaves your body when you breathe out.

cartilage material similar to bone but flexible. Cartilage covers and cushions the ends of bones at joints.

cell one of the tiny building blocks that all living things are made from. Your cells need energy to make them work.

circulation movement of blood. The network of blood vessels means your blood can circulate to every part of your body.

contract get smaller or shorter. A stretched rubber band contracts when you stop pulling it.

dehydration not having enough water. Dehydration can make you feel thirsty, sick, and headachy.

diaphragm sheet of muscle across the bottom of your chest. Your diaphragm helps you to breathe.

drug substance that affects the way your body works. Taking drugs is banned in many sports.

elastic can be stretched. A rubber band is elastic.

expand get bigger or longer. A balloon expands when you blow it up.

fat type of food chemical or food group. Butter, oil, and fried foods all contain fats.

flexible can be bent. A training shoe is flexible.

heart organ that pumps blood around your body. Your heart pumps non-stop, even when you are asleep.

interval training swapping between two different types of exercise. If you run, walk, run, walk, run, walk you are doing interval training.

joint place where two bones meet. Your joints allow your body to bend.

lactic acid substance that your muscles make when they work hard. Cooling down lets your muscles get rid of lactic acid.

ligament strong band that holds a joint together. Without ligaments your joints would be weak and wobbly.

lungs organs that you use for breathing. Your lungs take in air and let out waste gases.

mineral useful chemical found in food. Iron and salt are both minerals.

muscle part of your body that can move bones. Without muscles you would not be able to move at all.

nutrient part of your food that your body can use. Proteins and vitamins are both nutrients.

oxygen gas that your body needs to work. You get oxygen from the air when you breathe in.

pore tiny hole. Pores in your skin let sweat trickle out.

protein type of food chemical or food group. Proteins help to build body parts and repair our bodies. Meat, fish, eggs, and nuts all contain proteins.

pulse rate how fast your heart is beating. You can measure your pulse rate at your wrist.

resting rate your pulse rate when you are resting. It should be slow and steady.

ribcage bony cage in your chest. Your ribcage protects your heart and lungs.

skeleton all your bones together. Your skeleton is the framework for the rest of your body.

spine bones in your back. Your spine is flexible and lets you twist and bend.

stamina being able to keep going for a long time. It takes a lot of stamina to run a marathon.

sweat glands parts of your skin that make you sweat. You have about 3 million sweat glands in your body!

thigh part of your leg between your hip and your knee. The thigh bone is the longest in your body.

vein type of blood vessel. Veins are bigger than capillaries but not as strong as arteries.

vitamin type of useful chemical found in food. For example, vitamin C is found in oranges.

windpipe tube that connects your mouth and nose to your lungs. Air passes through your windpipe when you breathe in and out.

Find out more

Books

Body Matters: Why Should I Get Off the Sofa? And Other Questions About Health and Exercise, Louise Spilsbury (Heinemann Library, 2004)

Get Fit! Eat Right! Be Active!: Girls Guide to Health & Fitness, Michelle H. Nagler (Scholastic, 2001)

Healthy Body: Exercise and Your Body, Polly Goodman (Hodder Wayland, 2005)

Keeping Healthy: Exercise, Carol Ballard (Hodder Wayland, 2007)

Kid Power: Active Kids, Bobbie Kalman (Crabtree Publishing Co, 2003)

Training for the Top: Nutrition and Energy, Paul Mason (Raintree, 2005)

What About Health: Exercise, Fiona Waters (Hodder Wayland, 2004)

Websites

http://news.bbc.co.uk/cbbcnews/hi/specials/sport/sportsround/default.stm

Read up-to-date news on different sports, and find out how you can get involved.

www.kidshealth.org

You can find the answers to many questions about keeping fit and healthy on this website.

Organizations

British Gymnastics

British Gymnastics, Ford Hall, Lillehall NSC, Newport, Shropshire, TF10 9NB
www.british-gymnastics.org

British Swimming and Amateur Swimming Association

The ASA is involved with swimming at every level, from beginners to Olympic standard.
ASA, Harold Fern House, Derby Square, Loughborough, Leicestershire, LE11 5AL
www.britishswimming.org

England Athletics

England Athletics, Athletics House, Central Boulevard, Blythe Valley Park,
Solihull, West Midlands, B90 8AJ
www.british-athletics.co.uk

English Federation of Disability Sport

The national body responsible for developing sport for disabled people in England.
English Federation of Disability Sport, Manchester Metropolitan University,
Alsager Campus, Hassall Road, Alsager, Stoke on Trent, ST7 2H
www.efds.net

Index

Leisure & Community Services

Please return this item by the last date stamped below, to the library from which it was borrowed.

Renewals

You may renew any item twice (for 3 weeks) by telephone or post, providing it is not required by another reader. *Please quote the number stated below.*

Overdue charges

Please see library notices for the current rate of charges for overdue items. Overdue charges are not made on junior books unless borrowed on adult tickets.

Postage

Both adult and junior borrowers must pay any postage on overdue notices.

5/04	WITHDRAWN FROM	
24 SEP 2005	BROMLEY LIBRARIES	
15 OCT 16		
5 NOV LV		
29 AUG 2015		
2 4 AUG 2019		

739.96

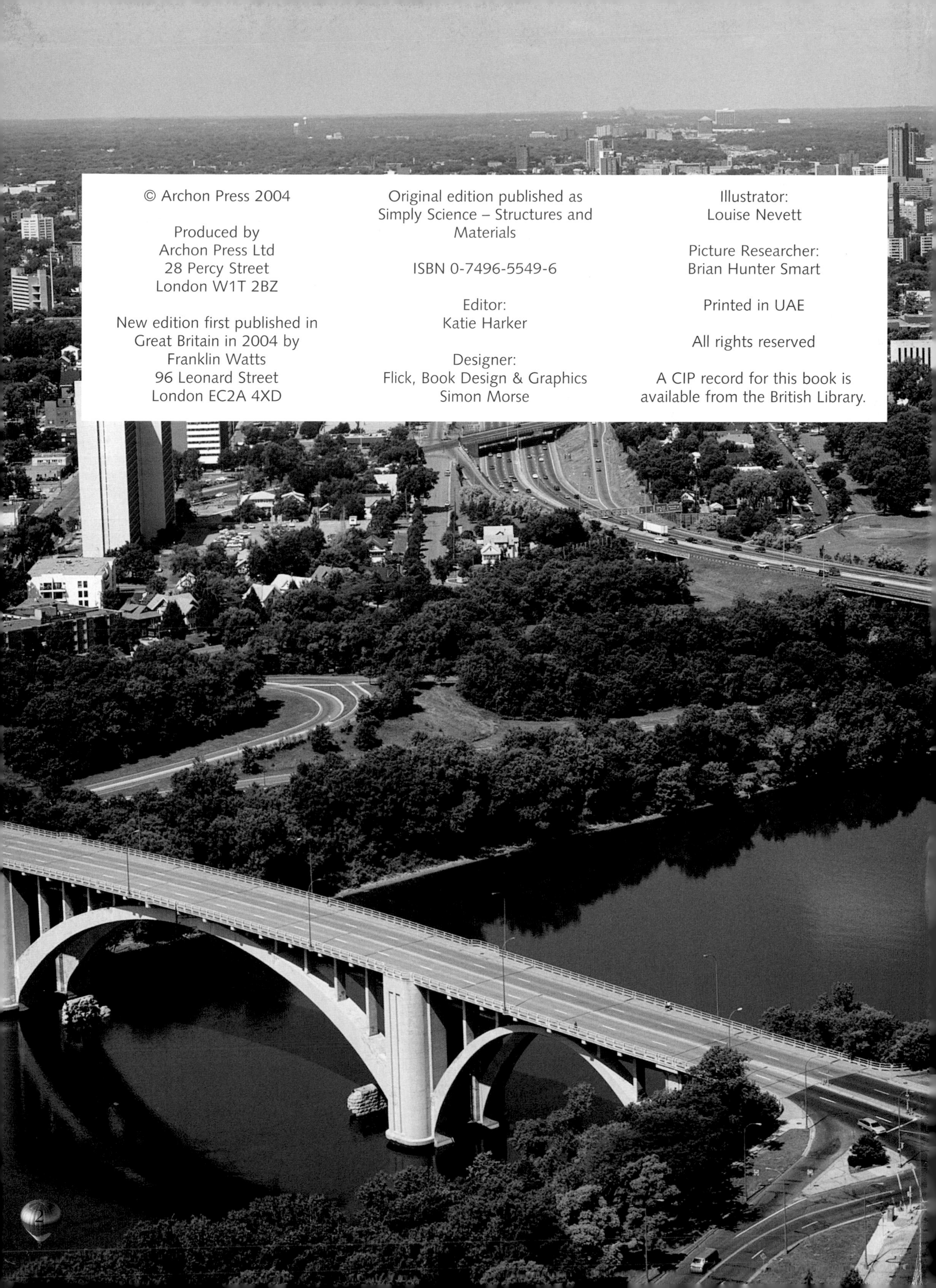

© Archon Press 2004

Produced by
Archon Press Ltd
28 Percy Street
London W1T 2BZ

New edition first published in
Great Britain in 2004 by
Franklin Watts
96 Leonard Street
London EC2A 4XD

Original edition published as
Simply Science – Structures and
Materials

ISBN 0-7496-5549-6

Editor:
Katie Harker

Designer:
Flick, Book Design & Graphics
Simon Morse

Illustrator:
Louise Nevett

Picture Researcher:
Brian Hunter Smart

Printed in UAE

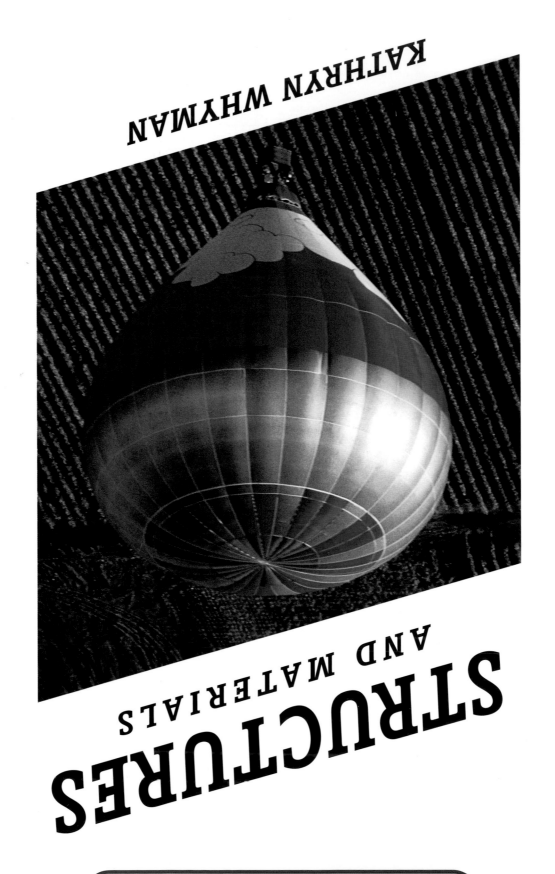

KATHRYN WHYMAN

STRUCTURES
AND MATERIALS

Franklin Watts
London • Sydney

SCIENCE WORLD

When water freezes, its molecules spread further apart to form crystals of ice or snow.

Carbon fibre, used to make this boat, is tougher than steel because its molecules have strong bonds.

LIVING STRUCTURES

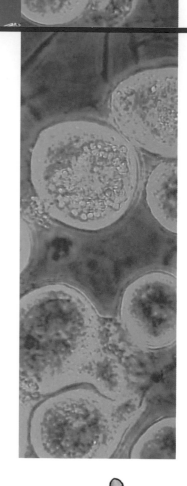

Living things are made of 'cells' – tiny structures which you can only see with the aid of a microscope, though each cell contains millions of molecules! Human and animal cells are soft – they do not provide support or give a definitive shape. Instead, humans and animals have a skeleton of bones which supports the body, protects delicate organs and helps the body to move.

Plants do not need a skeleton of bones. Each of their cells is surrounded by a 'wall' of material called 'cellulose'. As long as the cells have enough water they can support the plant. Some special cells form 'veins' through the plant, which help to transport water and nutrients.

The diagram shows a section through a vein in a leaf. You can see that the leaf is made up of different types of cells. Cells on the leaf surface are wax-coated to stop the leaf drying out. The cells which make up the veins carry food and water around the plant, as well as providing support.

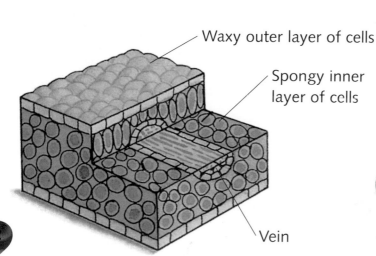

Waxy outer layer of cells

Spongy inner layer of cells

Vein

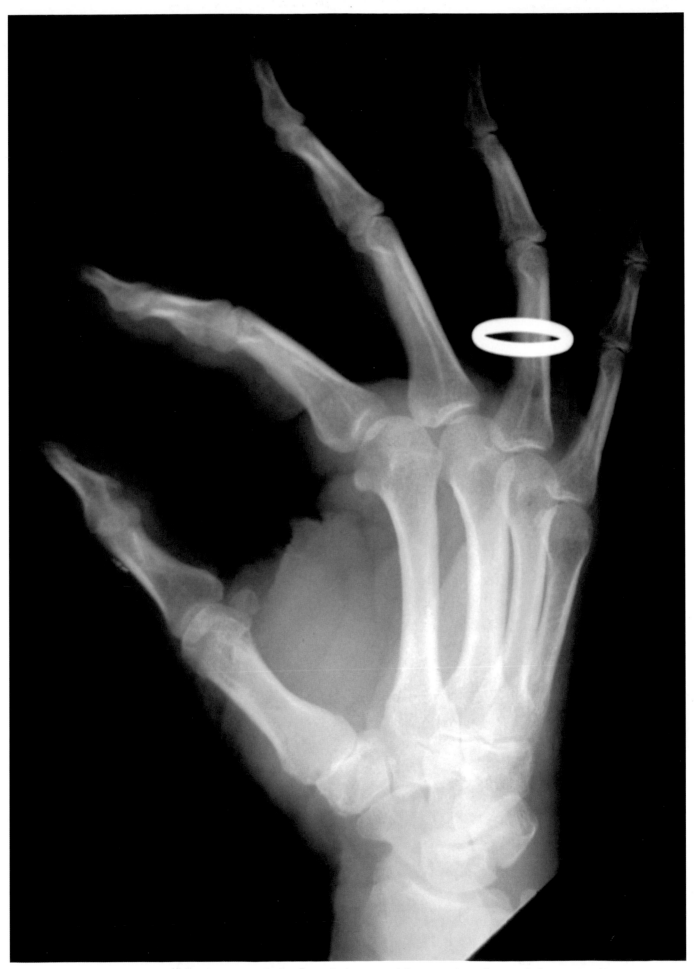

This X-ray shows the many bones of the hand that enable us to perform delicate tasks.

NATURAL MATERIALS

For centuries, materials that occur naturally in the world around us have been used to build everyday structures. Over the years, wood and stone proved to be reliable construction materials and gradually these materials have been used together to make more complex structures.

Some natural materials need to be purified (refined), separated or extracted before we can use them. Oil is refined to give a range of materials, from wax to petrol. Metals are separated from their ores and salt is separated from sea water or rock salt. Combining and treating natural materials can also produce artificial or 'man-made' materials.

 This pyramid, made of stone blocks, was built around 2600 BC, as a burial chamber for Egyptian kings.

Oil is extracted from beneath the Earth's surface.

Copper ore is the basis of many metal products.

Making glass

Glass is made mostly of sand – small, loose grains that come from rocks that have been weathered by the action of winds, rivers, waves or glaciers. The world's largest deposits of sand are found in the deserts and on beaches. Glass is made by mixing sand with soda ash and limestone. When these substances are heated in a furnace at high temperatures they melt and join together to make glass. Sand is also used extensively in the manufacture of bricks, mortar, cement, concrete, plaster and paving materials.

Sand

Glass

MAN-MADE MATERIALS

Today, many of our major industries are involved in the production of man-made materials. Look around and you will see numerous structures made from these. Steel, plastic and glass are all man-made materials that are manufactured from natural resources. Steel is made from iron; plastic is made from chemicals found in oil; and glass is mostly made from sand.

Man-made materials have been developed over the years because they have special properties suited for a particular job. Advances in technology have meant that today, in some cases, man-made materials are also easier and cheaper to manufacture.

Glass is perfect for making windows. Glass can also be blown or moulded into shapes, or thin fibres.

Plastics

Plastics are usually made from chemicals which come from oil. Plastics are cheap, easy to make, light and they do not rust or rot. For these reasons plastics are often used instead of metal, wood or glass. The properties of plastics vary according to their chemical structure. Some plastic structures, like these bags (right), are flexible. Others are rigid, transparent or strong.

These steel cables are strong and flexible. Steel can also be toughened by adding quantities of carbon.

CHOOSING THE RIGHT MATERIAL

Not only must a structure have the right shape, it must also be made of a suitable material. The material you choose will depend on its properties and the job that the structure is going to be used for.

It is sensible to make the windows of a house out of glass because it is transparent, and the walls out of bricks because they are strong. The cost of the material is also an important factor to think about. You may think that silk would be the best material to make dusters, but it would be rather a waste of money!

- Aluminium
- Steel
- Carbon fibre / reinforced plastic
- Fire-resistant materials
- Plastics
- Paint

Various materials have been chosen to make this aircraft. The framework is strong, the wings and body are light, the interior is colourful and the fittings are fire resistant and easily moulded.

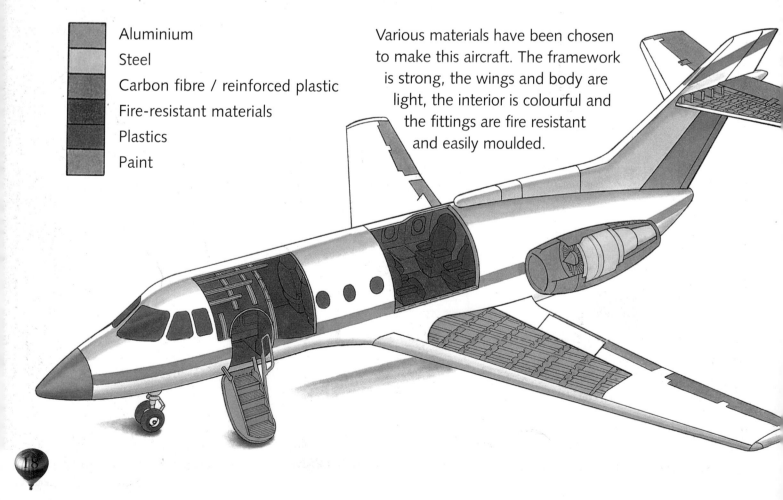

Different bicycle designs suit different purposes. A racing bike has slick tyres on narrow wheels while an off-road bike has fat tyres and a sturdy frame. Steel frames are cheap and relatively rust-resistant. Aluminium is a lighter alternative. Titanium is slightly flexible so it gives a smoother ride.

Carbon fibre is strong and flexible. It is used to make boat masts because it can withstand large forces.

RIGIDITY

You may have noticed that some animals, like giraffes or young foals, splay their legs as they try to stand upright. By making a triangle with their legs and the surface of the ground, they make themselves more stable. Tents are often designed with triangular frameworks for the same reason. This structure is less likely to collapse in windy weather. Triangular shapes are 'rigid' – they cannot change.

A strong structure also needs the right materials. The molecules of some solids are arranged in rigid patterns. These materials can only bend very slightly and are likely to break – they are 'brittle'. For this reason, a standard glass rod will break more easily than one made of steel.

Keeping stable

Three sticks can be joined together to form a triangle. The joints are pivoted but it is impossible to change the shape of the triangle unless you break it – it is rigid.

But if sticks are used to make a square, and you push the corners of the square to change its shape, or even flatten it, you can see that this shape is not rigid.

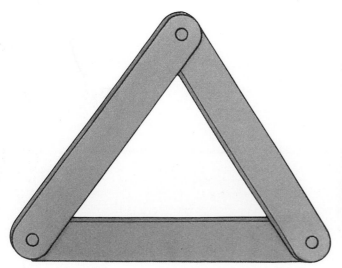

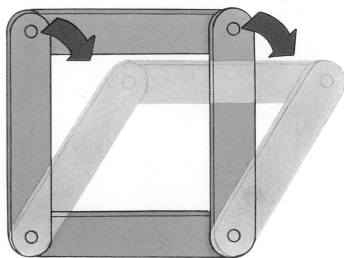

The triangular structure of the Eiffel Tower in Paris keeps it strong, sturdy and rigid.

FLEXIBILITY

Materials which bend or change shape when they are pushed or pulled are 'flexible'. Some materials, like rubber, are flexible because they are 'elastic'. You can stretch a rubber band, but it will return to its original shape when you let it go. Other materials, like metals, can return to their original shape even when a very large force is applied. These materials are useful for building strong structures.

Tall buildings are designed to be flexible and will sway a little in the wind. Trees are also flexible, although strong winds may sometimes stretch them too far! Even our bones are flexible while we are young. As we get older, they become more brittle and likely to break.

Diving boards are made from wood, fibreglass or aluminium. Fibreglass and aluminium make the most flexible boards, enabling a diver to jump high over the water before entry.

This rubber ball is a sphere. When it drops to the ground, the ground exerts a force on it and the ball changes shape. But as the ball bounces upwards and the force from the ground is removed, it once again becomes spherical. The rubber ball is elastic.

The flexible trunks of palm trees allow them to bend in the wind.

DENSITY AND STRUCTURES

If you hold a block of cork in one hand and a block of glass of exactly the same shape and size in the other, you will notice that the glass feels heavier than the cork. We say that glass is more 'dense' than cork.

But what makes some materials more dense than others? It may be that the molecules are heavier, or they may be packed more closely together. Solids are often more dense than liquids for this reason. Yet many solids are less dense than liquids. Ice, for example, floats on water because its molecules are further apart.

Birds are able to remain in the air easily as they fly. Their wings are specially designed for this purpose. One feature of the wings is that their bones contain large air spaces. Because these bones consist of the bone tissue and air, they are less dense than they would be if they were solid bone. This structure also makes the bones stronger and less likely to break.

Section through a wing bone

These balloons have been filled with hot air which is less dense than the cooler air outside.

STRUCTURES IN ACTION

All structures are designed to do particular jobs. Every structure of your body has its own shape – from the hard, sharp teeth you use for biting to the strong, flexible feet on which you walk. Every object in the room around you, however simple, also has a shape suitable for its purpose.

Some of the structures we build are very complicated. A bridge must support its own weight and the weight of the vehicles travelling across it. Suspension bridges literally hang from thick cables stretched over massive supports. Strong, taught wires join the bridge to the cables.

Light but strong

Aircraft wings are not made of solid metal – this would be too heavy. But they have to be strong. The insides of the wings are often made up of a framework of six-sided aluminium 'cells' filled with air.

Honey-bees have been using this sort of structure since long before aircraft were invented! Their honeycombs, which house their young and store their food, are strong and make good use of space.

Aluminium honeycomb structure used for aircraft

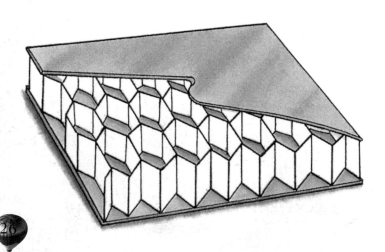

Bee honeycomb

Right: The Golden Gate suspension bridge, USA

Muscle

Tendon

Joint

Our skeleton is not a totally rigid structure – it has joints which allow us to move. This diagram shows the structure of an elbow joint. The joint is rather like the hinge on a door. Muscles, attached to the bones by strong tendons, contract (shorten) or relax (lengthen) to move the bones of the arm up or down.

MAKE YOUR OWN KITE

This kite is a simple structure which you can build from everyday materials – and it is fun to fly, too! Your kite must be made from light yet strong and flexible materials. Plastic is used to cover the frame which is made from light wood. It makes a light, strong structure.

A kite's special structure means that it can soar in the wind.

What you need
Two light sticks
A plastic bag
Cotton
A ball of string
Sheet of paper

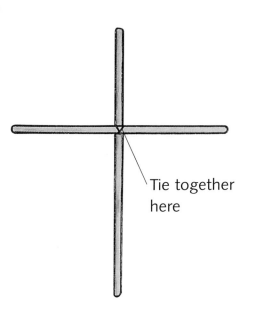

Tie together
here

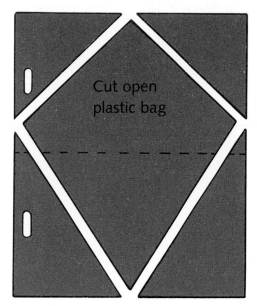

Cut open
plastic bag

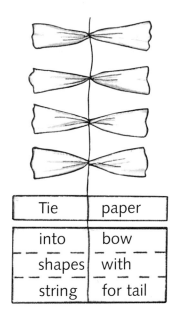

Tie	paper
into	bow
shapes	with
string	for tail

Make a framework by tying two sticks firmly together. This framework gives you the shape for your kite. Now cut open the plastic bag and cut out a piece to fit your framework. You can make your kite more balanced by giving it a tail of plastic (see photo, far left) or string and folded paper (see below left). Join all the parts of the kite together. The corners must be tied securely, first with cotton and then with string. Make sure the ball of string is attached to all four corners.

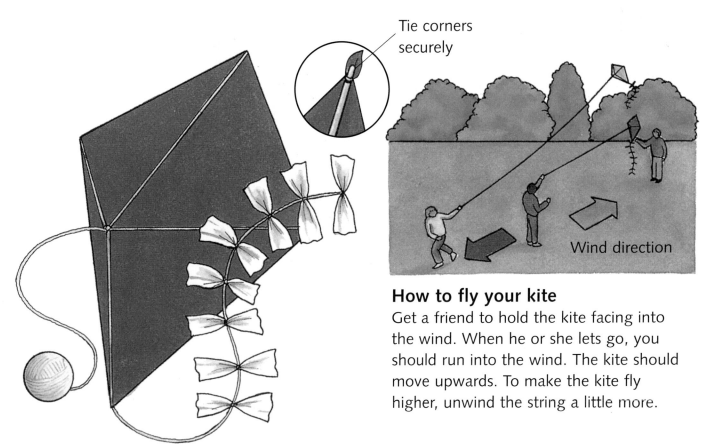

Tie corners
securely

Wind direction

How to fly your kite

Get a friend to hold the kite facing into the wind. When he or she lets go, you should run into the wind. The kite should move upwards. To make the kite fly higher, unwind the string a little more.

MORE ABOUT STRUCTURES

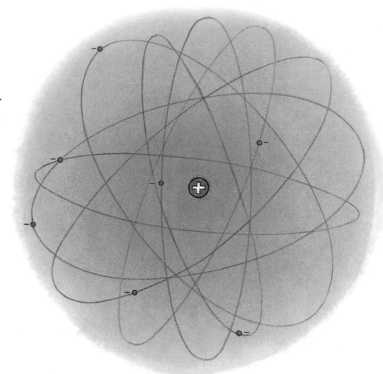

The structure of an atom

All atoms have the same basic structure. The central nucleus is the heaviest part of the atom. It is made up of two types of particle: neutrons and protons. Neutrons have no 'charge', but the protons each carry a positive charge. So the nucleus is shown with a plus sign.

Travelling around the nucleus are particles we call electrons. These particles have a negative charge, so we show them with a minus sign. Since the atom has the same number of positive and negative charges, they balance each other out. The atom is 'neutral'.

Bonding structures

Salt is made up of atoms of sodium and chlorine. When a pair of these atoms comes together, it behaves in a special way. One of the electrons belonging to the sodium atom moves towards the chlorine atom. Now the charges of the atoms are no longer balanced. The sodium atom has an extra positive charge and the chlorine has an extra negative charge. We call the sodium a positive 'ion' and the chlorine a negative ion. In salt, the sodium and chlorine ions are bonded together by a balance of these charges. This balance gives the salt molecule its cubic shape.

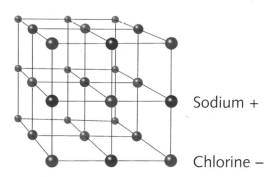

Sodium +

Chlorine −

GLOSSARY

Adhesive
A substance used for sticking objects together. Also called glue. Adhesives are often made from animal bones, hoofs and tree resins.

Atom
A tiny particle. It is the smallest part of an element that can exist and still have all the characteristics of that element.

Bond
The force which holds atoms together to form molecules.

Carbon fibre
A black silky thread of pure carbon made by heating and stretching textile fibres. Because of its lightness and strength at high temperatures, carbon fibre is used to reinforce materials such as plastic, metal and glass.

Cell
A very small part of living matter. Different kinds of cells do different jobs in the body of a plant or animal.

Cellulose
A natural substance made up of long chains of molecules. It forms the walls of plant cells.

Crystals
Formed when a pure substance becomes a solid. Crystals have a definite shape with edges, corners and flat surfaces.

Density
Mass compared to volume. Solids are often denser than liquids.

Electron
A tiny particle of matter in orbit around the nucleus of an atom. It has a negative electric charge.

Evaporate
To change a liquid into a gas, often by heating.

Hydrogen
A very light gas. Hydrogen atoms are also found in compounds such as water.

Materials
Substances from which something is made.

Molecule
Two or more atoms which exist as a group. A molecule is the smallest part of a compound which can exist on its own and still have all the characteristics of that compound.

Neutron
One of the tiny particles in the nucleus of all atoms (except hydrogen). Neutrons have no electric charge.

Nucleus
The centre of an atom, which contains tiny particles called protons and neutrons.

Ore
Any naturally occurring mineral from which metal can be extracted.

Oxygen
A colourless gas which makes up about a fifth of the air we breathe. Oxygen atoms are also found in a variety of other substances including water.

Properties
Characteristics which describe the appearance or behaviour of a substance in different conditions.

Proton
A tiny particle in the nucleus of all atoms. Protons have a positive charge.

Refined
Separated into various pure substances.

31